COMPUTERS

Written By:
Herbert I. Kavet

Illustrated By:
Martin Riskin

Ivory Tower Publishing Co., Inc.
125 Walnut Street
P.O. Box 9132
Watertown, MA 02272-9132
Telephone #: (617) 923-1111   Fax #: (617) 923-8839

"Honey, I think she's learning to use it."

How Computers Rot Your Brains

Most people think computers rot your brains by doing the calculations you used to use your head to figure out. This may be true, but computers really do their damage by:

1. Providing an overload of information in the form of reports.

2. They do this only on a monthly, or even more frequent, basis.

3. Because it's from a computer, the information appears to be accurate so you believe it.

4. The information has just enough totally stupid errors in it to render it completely useless.

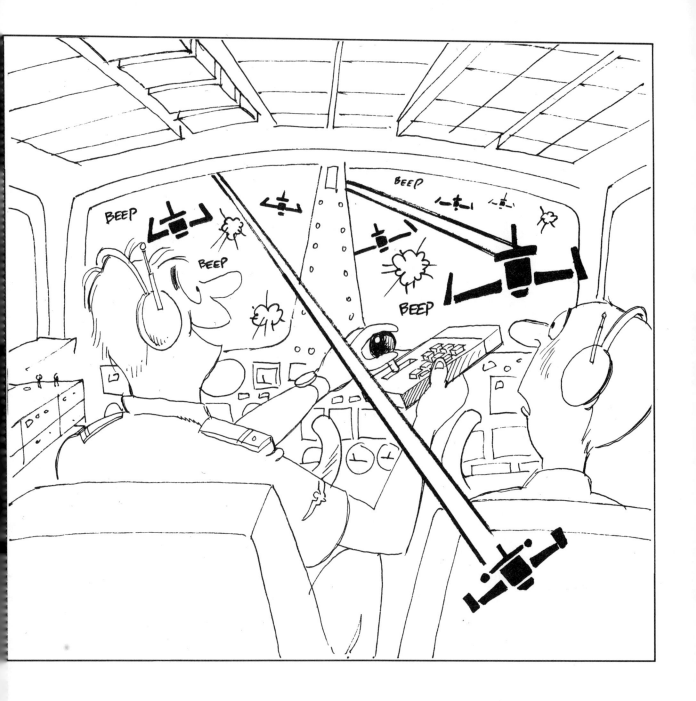

How Bugs Really Get Into Your Computer

Computer Commands You'd Better Respect

1. Do you really want to delete this file?

2. Report about to be printed requires 25,000 sheets of paper.

3. Format your hard drive.

Where Garbled Commands Really End Up

How Computers Think

As everyone knows, computers think by turning little switches on and off. This seems pretty silly but since computers can turn these little switches on and off very quickly, sort of like a 3-year-old playing with the first light switch he can reach, they can annoy the electrons into doing arithmetic. This doesn't happen with our average 3-year-old because they annoy their parents long before they get to the electrons.

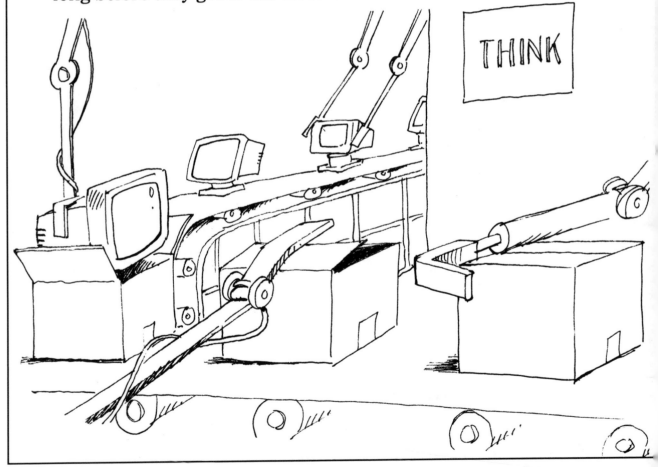

"If carpenters built buildings the way programmers write programs, then civilization would be destroyed by the first woodpecker to come along."

When writing programs, the first 90% of the projects take 90% of the time. The remaining 10% takes about four times longer.

"But Mr. Finkelstein, everyone knows data expands
to fill the hard disks available.

What Modems Really Do

Modems enable computers to talk to one another. Computers need to talk to one another because they are lonely. They're lonely because computers are, underneath their incredible arithmetic efficiency, basically unbelievably stupid creatures. Have you ever talked to a computer? I certainly hope not.

Computer Viruses

Everyone realizes that computer viruses are created by diabolical programming weirdos who derive intense joy from generating mischief with people's time. Thankfully, there are plenty of programs around to purge these viruses which are probably written by exactly the same kind of person. It's like buying medicine from a bacteria.

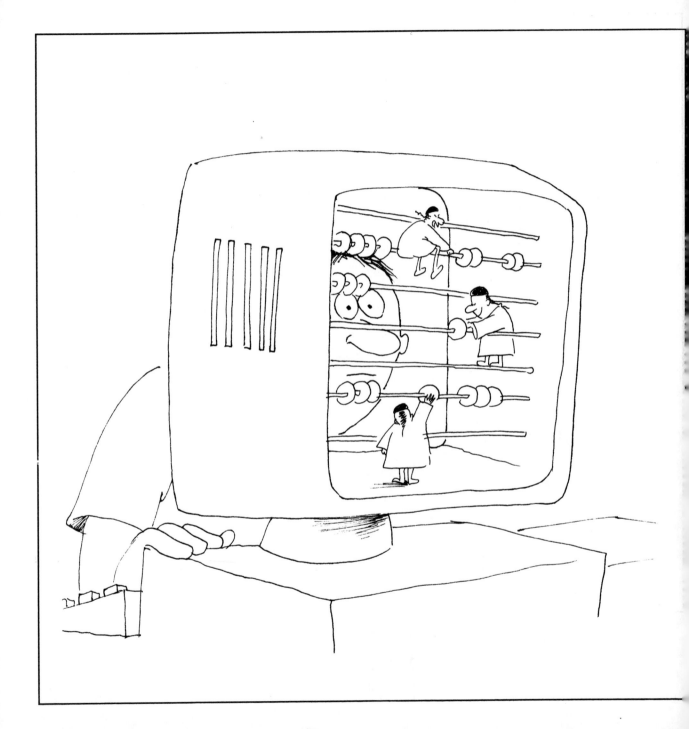

"This multi media is terrific. Now when I open my printouts I have a pornographic picture on every page and it plays Beethoven's 5th."

Laws of Programming

1. A smoothly running program is probably obsolete.

2. Any useful program will have to be updated.

3. Any given program costs more and takes longer.

4. It is better to start over than to transfer information from one system to another.

5. Any given program will expand to fill all available memory.

How to Buy a Computer

Buying a computer is easy. Go into a dark closet in the most remote corner of your basement and whisper, "I think I need a computer." By the time you return to your living room, at least four friends will have appeared, each an expert on some phase of computer operations totally different from what you are trying to accomplish and full of conflicting advice on which machine to buy.

How Computers Really Work

No one really knows how they REALLY work. Well, maybe my nephew David at MIT but almost no one else. I mean everyone knows basic binary systems and chips, and on and off, but how does all this print out spread sheets, or play interplanetary attack games? Any sufficiently advanced technology is indiscernible from magic, so you might as well figure computers work on magic and be done with it.

In a new job it's important to find the only person in an office who understands the computer. Make friends with this person.

"That new Apple is as user friendly as they come."

Selling Old Computers

Don't ever try to sell an old computer because it will only break your heart. Better, give them to a cousin or let the kids play with them out in the backyard. That electronic whiz that cost about $2,000,000 and came with a bevy of handlers and salesmen in a bullet proof shipping container will now cost a $60 "environmental charge" if you want them to haul it away.

Computers and Planes

I've never sat next to anyone on a plane that didn't work for a computer company. I mean these people must travel constantly. "And what do you do?" "Oh, I'm in system design" or "computer analysis" or "software development." And it must be even worse up in first class, but I wouldn't know.

Hard Disk Storage

Need to store the names and sexual preferences of everyone in the world? How about adding every book printed since the Gütenberg Bible to your lap top? No problem — just buy, for a little more than a case of beer, a hard disk drive with 60 trillion trigabytes of storage. And then tell me computers don't work by magic.

Where Computers are Made

The inner, inner really magic parts of a computer are all made in a little known Asian country by carefully trained teenagers. These kids become really nimble with their fingers by snacking on slippery pine nuts with chopsticks. I'm not making this up. Better to have these kids making computer innards than out smashing mailboxes or experimenting with back seat sex like our teenagers.

Computer Boxes

Computers come packed in the most clever shipping cartons.
When you open these ingenious boxes, you know it would take a
nuclear detonation to disturb the contents.

The problem then arises as to where to store these monuments of
foam padding and stiff fiber inserts. I mean in case you ever want
to ship a computer back, you need the box or the warranty will be
voided. So you stick the box in your attic or cellar, plus a similar
box for every accessory, and if you're like me, create a fire hazard
in your storage area the size of Montana.

"Adam's playing with his new magnet kit."

Thank you for calling Software World. Your call is important to us, so please stay on the line. "Beep"

"Honey, did you bother with a backup this morning?"

Why Computers Crash

When a computer thinks the information you are working with is really important, it says, " Hey, let's have some fun with this person" and the probability of a crash goes way up. Sophisticated operators will always try to convince the computer that the work they're doing is trivial.

"Marcia insists on scanning each of her dates into her diary."

How Trivial Information is Deleted

You: Delete this file
Computer: Do you really want to delete this file?
You: Yes
Computer: Type yes three times
You: Yes Yes Yes
Computer: What's your grandmother's maiden name?
You: Von Bletsky
Computer: Last chance to cancel deletion. ARE YOU SURE?
You: Dammit, YES!
Computer: Cross your heart?

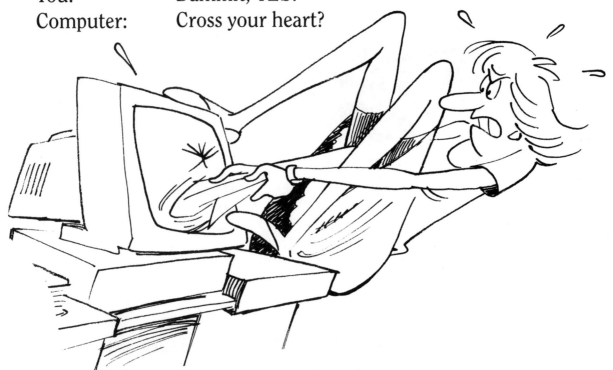

How Really Important Information is Deleted

The People Who Name Computer Components

"That laser jet printer just has a mind of its own."

"Leonardo – no one's going to respect that handwritten stuff."

Computer Manuals

Once there was a hacker named Henry who lived in Nebraska and understood computer manuals. Henry was a high school drop out who started building computers from bent paper clips and later was able to break into secret Pentagon computers and start brush fire wars with impunity. Anyhow, no one since then has really understood computer manuals and if you're smart you'll only buy programs your friends already have and can explain to you (As long as you're doing that you might as well save some money and copy the program but DON'T COPY THIS BOOK.).

Lap Tops and Palm Tops

These incredibly compact computers enable businessmen and women to take their friends' addresses and all sorts of computer games along on trips, and then they're able to play these games on planes, in hotels, and in bathrooms. Once a skier named Dean tried to do some actual work on his portable computer at a ski lodge but he was ostracized by all his friends until he returned to playing solitaire.

Phoning for Help

You have a problem with some software or a piece of hardware that doesn't work. Assume for a moment that when you call an 800 number for help you get to talk to a real person. What happens next? Well, first you're overcome with the thrill of contact with a real guru who is all wise and will soon save your problem, but next this person will immediately hit you with so much technical information that your problem will appear trivial and you will decide to ignore it.

Static electricity on the new large screen work station delays Kathy's lunch.

The Programmer

Ask a programmer if the machine can provide some specific new information. They will first list about a thousand things they can give you right away. Next they will patiently explain that with a little effort they can format the information into another thousand ways, none of which are quite what you want. Finally, they will admit they can do it but that it'll be faster if you did it by hand.

Answers from your Programmer

1. It's already in the system.
2. It'll take more storage space than you have.
3. Someone has already done it but we can't find it.
4. There'll be a new program for that on the market in a few months.
5. I'll think it over (they don't know).

Buying Computers at a Store

Entering a computer store is like entering a psychological boxing ring with a professional fighter. First the customer and salesperson probe and test each other.

"May I help you?"

"Oh, just looking. Do you have anything that can work with a Garfinkle analysis?"

Then the competition begins when the salesperson and customer close with each other and start throwing around acronyms that bounce back and forth with increasing fury:

"SIMMSOPTIPLOPS"

"DOS DATA BLOCK"

"COMOUSEDRIV"

"FLAVIL"

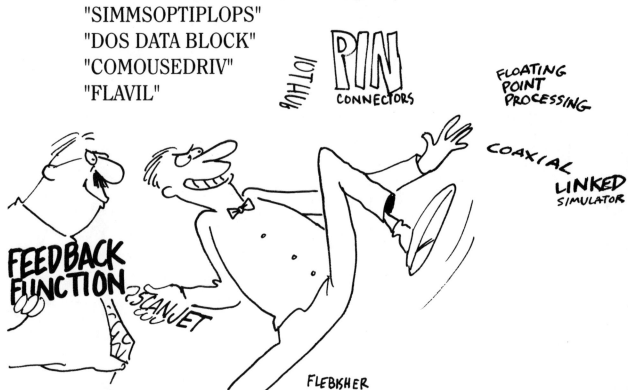

Buying Computers at a Store

The salesperson will usually win these acronym hurling contests 'cause they have been better trained and will send the customer off with their purchase and a promise of endless support to help solve whatever problems arise. This is true only until your check clears or until they leave to become a used-car salesman.

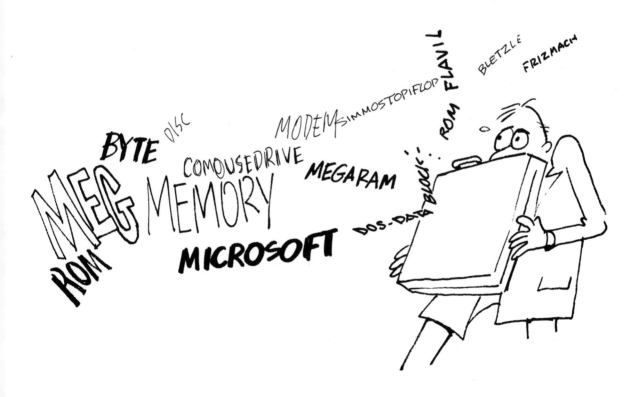

Printers

If you leave the room (or sometimes even look away) when a printer is printing, one of the following will happen:

1. It'll run out of paper.

2. The paper will jam.

3. It will compress your entire report onto one line.

Computer nerds go to a screen-saver party.

Computer Definitions

Password – a secret code that is forgotten almost immediately after it is installed

Spellcheck – an incredible system that proves just how ridiculous your 3rd grade teacher's priorities were

State of Art– a very brief moment in time between your purchase of a computer and the improved model's introduction at a lower price

Computer Definitions

New Version – a modern system for introducing viruses and bugs into your computer

On Line Help – a system for taking up memory with instructions you can't use

Font – name of an insidious style of letters conceived by software companies to entice users to buy so their literature can look like 18th century ads.

These other books are available at many fine stores.

#2350 Sailing. Using the head at night • Sex & Sailing • Monsters in the Ice Chest • How to look nautical in bars and much more nautical nonsense.

#2351 Computers. Where computers really are made • How to understand computer manuals without reading them • Sell your old $2,000,000 computer for $60 • Why computers are always lonely and much more solid state computer humor.

#2352 Cats. Living with cat hair • The advantages of kitty litter • Cats that fart • How to tell if you've got a fat cat.

#2353 Tennis. Where do lost balls go? • Winning the psychological game • Catching your breath • Perfecting wood shots.

#2354 Bowling. A book of bowling cartoons that covers: Score sheet cheaters • Boozers • Women who show off • Facing your team after a bad box and much more.

#2355 Parenting. Understanding the Tooth Fairy • 1000 ways to toilet train • Informers and tattle tales • Differences between little girls and little boys • And enough other information and laughs to make every parent wet their beds.

#2356 Fitness. T-shirts that will stop them from laughing at you • Earn big money with muscles • Sex and Fitness • Lose weight with laughter from this book.

#2357 Golf. Playing the psychological game • Going to the toilet in the rough • How to tell a real golfer • Some of the best golf cartoons ever printed.

#2358 Fishing. Handling 9" mosquitoes • Raising worms in your microwave oven • Neighborhood targets for fly casting practice • How to get on a first name basis with the Coast Guard plus even more.

#2359 Bathrooms. Why people love their bathroom • Great games to help pass the time on toilets • A frank discussion of bathroom odors • Plus lots of other stuff everyone out of diapers should know.

#2360 Biking. Why the wind is always against you • Why bike clothes are so tight • And lots of other stuff about what goes thunk, thunk, thunk when you pedal.

#2361 Running. How to "go" in the woods • Why running shoes cost more than sneakers • Keeping your lungs from bursting by letting the other guy talk.

Ivory Tower Publishing Co., Inc.   125 Walnut St., PO Box 9132, Watertown, MA 02272-9132
Telephone #: (617) 923-1111   Fax #: (617) 923-8839